lovable

A JOURNAL FOR PRACTICING SELF-LOVE & EMBRACING THE IRRESISTIBLE PERSON YOU ARE

nadia hayes

CASTLE POINT BOOKS
NEW YORK

www.castlepointbooks.com

The Castle Point Books trademark is owned by Castle Point Publishing, LLC.
Castle Point books are published and distributed by St. Martin's Press.

ISBN 978-1-250-22890-1 (trade paperback)

Design by Tara Long

Images used under license by Shutterstock.com

Our books may be purchased in bulk for promotional, educational, or business
use. Please contact your local bookseller or the Macmillan Corporate and
Premium Sales Department at 1-800-221-7945, extension 5442, or by email at
MacmillanSpecialMarkets@macmillan.com.

First Edition: January 2020

10 9 8 7 6 5 4 3 2 1

INTRODUCTION

To look upon others and know what makes them *lovable* is easy. A close friend, a trusted confidant, or a family member—the energy they emit shines on us in soul-nourishing rays and the result is something glowing, something pure. We take that feeling and have certainty that no matter the mountain they may need to climb or the sadness they may endure, they are worthy of love. We see their accomplishments and their spirit and feel a sense of awe. It's not always the case that we turn that lens back upon ourselves.

Lovable is a guided journal to magnify the love you owe yourself. Through mindful practice, thoughtful journaling prompts, and a bit of inspiration, you will have the opportunity to practice self-love regularly, meaningfully, and wholeheartedly. Remind yourself of the qualities that make you unique, that bring joy to others, and that bring confidence to your being. Open the shades and let love shine on the dark corners of your emotions. Embrace the wonderful you, then welcome the opportunity to show yourself unrelenting kindness. Let yourself be loved, because *you are lovable*.

who looks outside,
DREAMS;
who looks inside,
AWAKES.

—CARL JUNG

Soul Sunrise

AWAKEN TO YOUR INTERNAL BEAUTY. When you take the time to look inward, what are you surprised to find? What elements of your being can you take more time to nurture? While the world outside is worth dreaming about, the one within you is unmatched and just waiting for dawn.

Radiant Reflections

OPEN YOUR ARMS WIDE TO THE PERSON LOOKING BACK AT YOU IN THE MIRROR. Open your heart to the soul that reflects back at you. Who or what is keeping you from feeling full? Identify something positive about yourself that you accept completely, that you love unconditionally. Stand in front of the mirror and say it aloud and consider how it makes you feel.

because one
believes in oneself,
ONE DOESN'T TRY
TO CONVINCE OTHERS.
because one is
content with oneself,
ONE DOESN'T NEED
OTHERS' APPROVAL.
because one
accepts oneself,
THE WHOLE WORLD
ACCEPTS HIM OR HER.

—LAO TZU

TO LOVE ONESELF
IS THE BEGINNING OF A LIFELONG ROMANCE.

—OSCAR WILDE

Heart Full

LOVE YOURSELF TODAY AND EVERY DAY. How can you be your most supportive partner? What would you tell someone you love that you need to hear from yourself today? Think on the acts of love, sharing, and support that you give to other people. Turn that inward for a moment, and consider how you feel when you fill your heart with the love you give yourself.

Find the love you seek,
by first finding
the love within yourself.
LEARN TO REST IN THAT
PLACE WITHIN YOU
THAT IS YOUR TRUE HOME.

—SRI SRI RAVI SHANKAR

A Sense of Home

LOVE IS A PLACE TO CALL HOME. It resides within you, and it can be found outside of yourself for the comforts you seek. What love within you gives you peace? In what ways are you your own sense of comfort? Explore the possibility that home and love are right where you are. What does that mean to you?

I CELEBRATE MYSELF,
AND SING MYSELF.

—WALT WHITMAN

Soul Celebration

IT'S YOUR PARTY, AND IT'S YOUR TIME TO SING YOUR OWN PRAISES.
Imagine your life as if your participation in it were confetti. As you scatter yourself around the room, what colors do you bring to the festivities? Make a list of the many confetti qualities within yourself that bring joy to others.

WHEN ADMIRING
OTHER PEOPLE'S GARDENS,
don't forget to tend
to your own flowers.

—SANOBER KHAN

SECRET GARDEN

AS YOU STAND IN FRONT OF ANOTHER PERSON'S GARDEN GATE, peering at their beauty in full blossom, the intricate vines of their lives, and the opportunities that seem to burst into bloom before them, remember your own secret garden. In what ways is your life lush? Is your garden manicured or wild? Shower yourself in sunlight and rain through positive self-care. What makes *you* blossom?

UNOPENED GIFTS

NOT ALL GIFTS PRESENT THEMSELVES ON TIME or with clear direction about how to use them. A talent, a knack, or a sharp eye for something could be a landmark on your journey of self-exploration. No matter how insignificant, which personal gifts could you embrace more? How do they add to the scenery of your life?

WE ARE EACH GIFTED IN A
UNIQUE AND IMPORTANT WAY.
It is our privilege and our
adventure to discover
our own special light.

—MARY DUNBAR

Whatever you are doing,
LOVE YOURSELF FOR DOING IT.

Whatever you are feeling,
LOVE YOURSELF FOR FEELING IT.

—THADDEUS GOLAS

A Loving Path

APPRECIATE THE PATH YOU ARE ON, BE IT ROCKY OR SMOOTH. What are the feelings that trouble you the most—the ones that you find yourself making excuses for? Whenever you find yourself qualifying a feeling by saying something like, "This is crazy of me," or "I should get over this," take a moment to consider the process. In what ways is the churn of those feelings helping you through to the other side?

SOMETIMES YOU
HAVE TO BE ALONE
TO TRULY KNOW
YOUR WORTH.

—KAREN A. BAQUIRAN

THE VALUE of I

OPPORTUNITIES FOR INDEPENDENCE WILL GREET YOU IN DIFFERENT DISGUISES. Whether you feel alone in a romantic sense, alone in your professional efforts, or alone in an opinion, those are moments that are full of unburdened possibility. Don your alone time with enthusiasm—how do you feel alone? What parts of yourself become emboldened that may not otherwise?

NO STAR IS EVER LOST
WE ONCE HAVE SEEN;
we always may be what
we might have been.

—ADELAIDE ANNE PROCTER

Always in Your Orbit

THE STARS ARE WITHIN YOUR REACH. As your days turn—time and again—upon the axis beneath your feet, it can feel as if the things you most want or the hopes you have are farther and farther behind you. But with each passing day, these opportunities will circle back around, if only you'd look up. What bright light within yourself is always there, just waiting for its moment to shine?

FRIENDSHIP WITH ONE'S SELF IS ALL IMPORTANT,

because without it
one cannot be friends
with anyone else
in the world.

—ELEANOR ROOSEVELT

A Friend in Me

BECOME CLOSER TO THE FRIEND WITHIN YOU. Make a list of the qualities in yourself that make you a good friend. Whether you are a good listener, a good helper, or good at cracking a joke, turn those qualities inward.
How can you be the best friend to yourself that you want to be to others?

A STORYBOOK LIFE

YOUR STORY IS YOURS TO LIVE. Every story can have darkness, fear, and, at times, tragedy. But that's not all. When something in your story goes awry, how will you write the next pages? Write about something meaningful to you and outline a hopeful next chapter.

A person's tragedy does not make up their entire life.
A STORY CARVES DEEP GROOVES INTO OUR BRAINS EACH TIME WE TELL IT.
But we aren't one story.
WE CAN CHANGE OUR STORIES.

—AMY POEHLER

YOUR TASK IS NOT
TO SEEK FOR LOVE,
but merely to seek
and find all the barriers
within yourself that you
have built against it.

—RUMI

LET LOVE IN

LOVE WILL KNOCK ON THE MANY DOORS OF YOUR HEART. Sometimes the knock is loud and makes its presence known, and other times it's a soft tap that could go unnoticed. You may be uncertain of what's on the other side. What kind of barriers have you put between yourself and love? How can you begin the process of unlatching those doors to let them swing wide open?

I WILL NOT
LET ANYONE
WALK THROUGH
MY MIND WITH
THEIR DIRTY FEET.

—MAHATMA GANDHI

Sacred Space

LET YOUR THOUGHTS ROAM FREE IN THE SACRED SPACE OF YOUR MIND.
When negative thoughts enter, show them the way out. What kinds of
negative thoughts do you or others try to put in your mind? What positive
ones can occupy the space they leave behind?

LIVE LIFE OUT LOUD

WHAT MAKES YOU FEEL MOST ALIVE? Whether it's finding exhilaration in the wind in your hair, dancing in the rain, or singing at the top of your lungs, there is something inside that feels like your secret life force. Wield that power—write about it here, and describe how you can harness it in your every day.

Don't ask yourself
what the world needs,
ask yourself what
makes you come alive.
AND THEN GO AND DO THAT.
Because what the world
needs is people
who have come alive.

—HOWARD WASHINGTON THURMAN

AS WE LET OUR
OWN LIGHT SHINE,
we unconsciously
give other people
permission to do
the same.

—MARIANNE WILLIAMSON

SHINE BRIGHT

ENERGY IS RECIPROCAL. What you put out encourages other people to reflect the same, whether toward you or those around you. Shine your inner light—appreciate the gifts you have and share them with others. Draw or write about your inner light below. How can you make it glow?

What lies behind us
AND WHAT LIES BEFORE US
are tiny matters compared to
WHAT LIES WITHIN US.

—RALPH WALDO EMERSON

Loving Direction

DRAW A ROADMAP OF YOUR HEART. Chart loving moments as landmarks to enjoy, and heartbreaks as pit stops. What kind of mileage do you get out of the love you have for yourself? How does your love for others keep you going?

LOVE IN THE PRESENT

PRACTICE SELF-LOVE WITH PURPOSE. What can you do today to show yourself true love? Assume you won't have time tomorrow and instead focus on the moments right in front of you. Cherish a moment with yourself and consider what that does for your heart.

ALL WE HAVE IS TODAY.
Just live it.
WE DON'T KNOW
ABOUT TOMORROW.
So, enjoy the day.
LOVE YOURSELF, AND
SPREAD LOVE AROUND.

—CHARLOTTE RAE

My mission in life is
not merely to survive,
BUT TO THRIVE;
and to do so with
SOME PASSION,
some compassion,
SOME HUMOR,
and some style.

—MAYA ANGELOU

THRIVE

WHEN EVERYTHING ELSE FEELS LIKE IT'S IN A DROUGHT, what is your oasis? Whether it's a person, an activity, or an act of self-care, find what brings you the sense of respite from a harsh day and let yourself feel nourished.

I will love the light
for it shows me the way,
YET I WILL ENDURE THE
DARKNESS BECAUSE IT
SHOWS ME THE STARS.

—OG MANDINO

CoSMIC GLoW

SCATTER YOUR MOMENTS AMONG THE STARS. When times were dark, what were the bright lights that shined through? What rays of light guided you out of the darkness?

SET SAIL

YOU CAN'T CONTROL THE ELEMENTS AS YOU NAVIGATE TOWARD A GOAL OR AN EMOTIONAL DESTINATION. Winds will pick up, storms can come, but you can adapt to make it through. When something or someone has thrown you off course, what emotional tools have you used to chart the course ahead?

I CAN'T CHANGE
THE DIRECTION
OF THE WIND,
BUT I CAN ADJUST MY SAILS
TO ALWAYS REACH
MY DESTINATION.

—JIMMY DEAN

HEALTH
is the greatest possession.

CONTENTMENT
is the greatest treasure.

CONFIDENCE
is the greatest friend.

—LAO TZU

Count Your Treasures

PERSONAL BLESSINGS CAN BE FOUND EVERYWHERE. In the circles below, jot down the things you appreciate about your body, your spirit, and the path you're on. What are you most grateful for? What small characteristics or feelings do you take for granted?

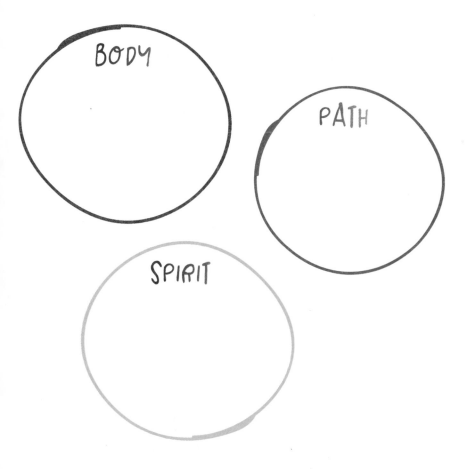

BODY

PATH

SPIRIT

Your present
circumstances
don't determine
where you can go;
THEY MERELY DETERMINE
WHERE YOU START.

—NIDO QUBEIN

WHERE *You* ARE AND WHERE *You* WILL Go

HERE AND NOW ARE TEMPORARY. This knowledge makes good moments worth cherishing and makes bad moments worth pushing through. What about your present circumstances makes you feel stuck? What about them makes you excited about the future?

CIRCLES of LOVE

HAPPINESS IS A GIFT OF LOVE TO BE SHARED. Feel the love radiating from the happiness around you, and share that love with others when you feel it, too. In the diagram below, write out how it might feel to others when you are radiating happiness, how it feels when their happiness shines upon you, and how it feels when the moment is created together.

WHOEVER
IS HAPPY
WILL MAKE
OTHERS
HAPPY TOO.

—ANNE FRANK

WE
ACCEPT
THE
LOVE
WE
THINK
WE
DESERVE.

—STEPHEN CHBOSKY

WORTHY

YOU ARE WORTHY OF LOVE. In times of internal turmoil, it can be difficult to accept love from others. How have others shown you love? Have you always accepted it, or have you pushed it away? Count the ways you can embrace that love in the future. How will it feel to let love in?

BE HERE NOW

BREATHE IN A QUIET MOMENT. Close your eyes and let the thoughts of your mind settle to a tranquil hum. How does it feel to sit with yourself in stillness? What about this private moment fills you with peace?

BREATHE. LET GO.
AND REMIND YOURSELF
THAT THIS VERY MOMENT
IS THE ONLY ONE YOU
KNOW YOU HAVE FOR SURE.

—OPRAH WINFREY

Find joy in everything
you choose to do.
EVERY JOB,
RELATIONSHIP, HOME...
it's your responsibility
to love it, or change it.

—CHUCK PALAHNIUK

A Joyful Heart

THERE ARE MYRIAD QUALITIES OF JOY IN EVERY FACET OF YOUR LIFE.
Some pieces of joy are harder to unearth, but you can find them if only
you dig a little beneath the surface. Find the bliss in the different terrains
of your life below, and focus on what they bring you.

HOME

FAMILY

LOVE

FRIENDSHIP

CAREER

Soul Shimmer

WHAT ABOUT YOU SPARKLES? Looking from the outside in, see how your colors change in the light. Imagine how other people see your special qualities and let those reflections cast a glow on your soul.

PEOPLE ARE LIKE
STAINED-GLASS WINDOWS.
They sparkle and shine
when the sun is out, but
when the darkness sets in,
their true beauty
is revealed only if there
is light from within.

—ELISABETH KÜBLER-ROSS

You find peace
not by rearranging
the circumstances
of your life,
BUT BY REALIZING
WHO YOU ARE AT
THE DEEPEST LEVEL.

—ECKHART TOLLE

DEEPEST PEACE

SOME CHANGES NEED TO BE MADE TO IMPROVE THE WELLNESS OF YOUR CIRCUMSTANCES. But when internal restlessness sets in and you feel like something is wrong with who you are or what you are doing, take a closer look. What about yourself are you not allowing to just be? When you find yourself inclined to cast criticism, can you show yourself compassion instead?

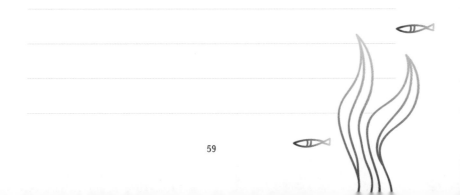

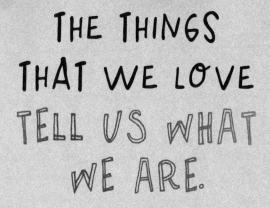

THE THINGS
THAT WE LOVE
TELL US WHAT
WE ARE.

—THOMAS AQUINAS

Love Acquired

IMAGINE THAT WHAT YOU LOVE IS CURRENCY. Add up the people, the experiences, and the things that fill you with love and feel their wealth in your heart. Who or what fills you with the most love? How do they feel your love in return?

SELFLESS SELF-CARE

NOURISH YOURSELF. Feed the hungry parts of your body and mind
with soulful sustenance. When the journey gets hard, take a break before
moving onward. In what ways can you follow your path to enrichment?
What acts of self-care sate your hunger?

I have come to believe
that caring for myself
is not self-indulgent.
CARING FOR MYSELF
IS AN ACT OF SURVIVAL.

—AUDRE LORDE

WHEN WE GIVE
OURSELVES
COMPASSION,
WE ARE OPENING
OUR HEARTS IN
A WAY THAT CAN
TRANSFORM
OUR LIVES.

—KRISTIN NEFF

AFFECTION REFLECTIONS

LOVE YOURSELF AS YOU LOVE OTHERS. Show yourself the compassion you would show a friend. Be kind to yourself as you would to someone in need. Give yourself affection as you would to someone you love. Describe how turning the love you give to others inward could fill you with warmth or contentment.

FIND WHAT MAKES YOUR HEART SING AND CREATE YOUR OWN MUSIC.

—MAC ANDERSON

HEART ON KEY

FOLLOW THE TUNE OF YOUR HEART, THE BEAT OF YOUR OWN DRUM.
Write or copy down a song verse that makes your heart sing. Hum the
melody as you pass over the words, and let yourself feel its soulful tune
from within.

To Love List

LOVING OTHERS IS AN ESSENTIAL PART OF HAPPINESS. But to engage well with the loved ones around you, you must love yourself first. Make a list of actions to take each day to show yourself love.

LOVE YOURSELF FIRST
AND EVERYTHING ELSE
FALLS INTO LINE.
You really have to love
yourself to get anything
done in this world.

—LUCILLE BALL

GIVE YOUR STRESS WINGS,

and let it fly away.

—TERRI GUILLEMETS

See You Soar

STRESS CAN SEEP INTO YOUR HEART, YOUR MIND, AND YOUR SPIRIT.
How does your stress affect your perception of yourself? Does your stress affect the people you love? When it starts to close in on you, give it a flight path. Write about how you can release the stress your carry into the wind.

IF ONLY YOU COULD
SENSE HOW IMPORTANT
YOU ARE TO THE LIVES
OF THOSE YOU MEET;
HOW IMPORTANT YOU CAN
BE TO PEOPLE YOU MAY
NEVER EVEN DREAM OF.
THERE IS SOMETHING OF
YOURSELF THAT YOU LEAVE
AT EVERY MEETING WITH
ANOTHER PERSON.

—FRED ROGERS

Footprints of the Self

YOU LEAVE FOOTPRINTS OF YOURSELF EVERYWHERE YOU GO, upon every life you touch. What do these prints look like? What path do you leave through someone else's heart?

NEVER LET ME GO

MOMENTS THAT WOUND THE SPIRIT CAN BE HARD TO GET THROUGH.
When your spirit is attacked, whether by the actions of hurtful people or
the fallout of a bad situation, find ways to protect and heal it. How can you
reinvigorate your sense of self when you feel threatened? What gives you
the strength to hold on to it?

ONE'S DIGNITY
MAY BE ASSAULTED,
VANDALIZED
AND CRUELLY
MOCKED,
but it can
never be
taken away
unless it is
surrendered.

—MICHAEL J. FOX

LIGHTEN UP
ON YOURSELF.
NO ONE IS PERFECT.
GENTLY ACCEPT
YOUR HUMANNESS.

—DEBORAH DAY

PERFECT IMPERFECTIONS

RELISH THE IMPERFECTIONS YOU SEE WITHIN YOURSELF. In one column, write a list of the characteristics you might otherwise be inclined to critique or feel negatively about. In the opposite column, write what there is to love about these beautifully human imperfections.

No other love
no matter how
genuine it is,
can fulfill one's
heart better than
UNCONDITIONAL
SELF—LOVE.

—EDMOND MBIAKA

LoVING KINDNESS

LOVE PERSISTS WHERE FORGIVENESS ENTERS. In moments when you are hard on yourself, show yourself love even when you don't think you deserve it. Forgive yourself for what you feel has gone wrong. What keeps you from showing yourself love? For what do you most want to be forgiven?

FLUTTERS of FONDNESS

LET WORDS OF LOVE FLUTTER AROUND YOUR HEART. Breathe in the fresh, crisp air of this season of love, and let encouragement whirl around you. Write out the words you most need to hear.

THERE ARE DAYS
I DROP WORDS OF COMFORT
ON MYSELF LIKE FALLING LEAVES

and remember that
it is enough to be
taken care of by myself.

—BRIAN ANDREAS

LOVE IS THE GREAT MIRACLE CURE.

Loving ourselves works miracles in our lives.

—LOUISE HAY

WHOLE-HEARTED HEALING

WHEN HAS BEING GOOD TO YOURSELF BEEN YOUR ANTIDOTE? Make a list of activities that you do for yourself that soothe you. What is it about them that makes you feel so good?

_____

_____

_____

_____

_____

_____

_____

_____

_____

_____

_____

_____

OWNING OUR STORY
and loving ourselves
through that process
IS THE BRAVEST THING
THAT WE'LL EVER DO.

—BRENÉ BROWN

DATE	SCENE	TAKE
TODAY	18	83

PRODUCTION

DIRECTOR YOU

CAMERA

ON SCREEN

IF YOU WERE TO PITCH YOUR LIFE STORY TO A FILM STUDIO, what kind of film would you hope it to be? Is it a romance, a thriller, a comedy, or even a brooding indie film? What about it do you most want to share?

KINDNESS ROCKS

ON THE KINDNESS ROCKS BELOW, write encouraging and sweet words to yourself in the same way you might for a friend. How would you describe yourself? What words do you most need to hear?

SELF-COMPASSION
is simply giving
the same kindness
to ourselves
that we would
give to others.

—CHRISTOPHER GERMER

Sometimes the
most important thing
in a whole day is
THE REST WE
TAKE BETWEEN
TWO DEEP BREATHS.

—ETTY HILLESUM

BREATHE IN PEACE

LET YOURSELF SIT STILL IN SILENCE or with the soothing sound of nature. Close your eyes, and breathe in deeply. Let your breath leave your mouth slowly and with purpose. Immerse yourself in this stillness and peaceful breathing for several minutes. What thoughts cross your mind? How does your body react to taking a moment of rest?

Your Cup Overfloweth

WHAT FILLS YOUR SPIRIT? Imagine your cup is in front of you. Fill it up as high as your spirits are feeling in this moment. Describe the source from which your cup fills. Is it a precious resource, or can you refill your cup more often?

When you
take time to
replenish your spirit,
it allows you
to serve others
from the overflow.
YOU CANNOT SERVE
FROM AN EMPTY VESSEL.

—ELEANOR BROWN

THERE IS NOTHING MORE
BEAUTIFUL THAN SEEING A
PERSON BEING THEMSELVES.

IMAGINE GOING THROUGH
YOUR DAY BEING
UNAPOLOGETICALLY YOU.

—STEVE MARABOLI

UNAPOLOGETICALLY WRITTEN

TREASURE THE QUALITIES THAT MAKE YOU UNIQUE. It is easy for the word "sorry" to become the weed that springs up in your linguistic garden, whether you are apologizing for something that is merely a difference in opinion, or as a way to fill the air when a situation is uncomfortable or unexpected. Write an unapologetic letter in which you embrace the things for which you might otherwise blurt out a *sorry*.

IT'S GOOD TO DO
UNCOMFORTABLE THINGS.
It's weight training
for life.

—ANNE LAMOTT

From Strange to Strength

DON'T LET YOUR SOUL ATROPHY. Begin strengthening it by exploring new possibilities. Which adventurous muscles have you yet to flex? What small things might take you out of your comfort zone? Begin small, slowly, and gradually. In one column, make a list of new exercises in excitement you'd be willing to try. On the opposite side, describe what you hope to learn or feel from it.

BIG LOVE

LOVE IS A VULNERABILITY. It strengthens and softens the heart at once. When you are most hurt, what acts of love help you through? When you feel the most love, what acts of love make you feel even more?

There is
no remedy
for love
BUT TO
LOVE MORE.

—HENRY DAVID THOREAU

Love in its essence
IS SPIRITUAL FIRE

—SENECA

AFLAME

STOKE THE FIRES WITHIN YOU. What makes your soul come alight? What kind of love do you hold inside you that could be used to warm others?

The most
powerful relationship
you will ever have
IS THE RELATIONSHIP
WITH YOURSELF.

—STEVE MARABOLI

MESSAGE IN A BOTTLE

WRITE YOURSELF A LOVE LETTER. Enchant and woo yourself in the way you would want someone to do for you. Explore what loving yourself might feel like, or what cherishing the relationship you have with yourself might do.

BEAUTIFUL ACCEPTANCE

IN THE SPACES BELOW, CONSIDER THE MOST BEAUTIFUL PARTS OF YOURSELF. The characteristics of which you are most proud or fond: describe them. In the other space, write about what you haven't accepted about yourself, or that somehow makes you feel a little bit lesser. Can you draw lines from one side of the page to the other? How might some of those feelings of insecurity connect to those of beauty?

BEAUTY
⬇

ACCEPTANCE
⬇

TO BE BEAUTIFUL
MEANS TO BE YOURSELF.
You don't need to be
accepted by others.
YOU NEED TO ACCEPT YOURSELF.

—THÍCH NHẤT HẠNH

Love is, in fact,
AN INTENSIFICATION OF LIFE,
a completeness,
A FULLNESS,
a wholeness of life.

—THOMAS MERTON

LIFE IN STEREO

WHEN HAVE YOU FELT MOST ALIVE? What elements of love were present in that moment? Whether there was something that led you to a feeling of exhilaration or a humbling moment in time, what changed in you after that moment? Consider its connection to love—love for yourself, love for the world around you, or love for others. Describe how that love feels to you now.

Your soul knows
the geography
of your destiny
BETTER THAN YOU DO.

—JOHN O'DONOHUE

RELEASE THE WHEEL

SOME THINGS CAN BE CONTROLLED, but the course of your life is not one of them. What pieces of your life are you trying to control that you should loosen your grip upon? What milestones ahead or feelings are you trying to steer toward, but without success? Allow yourself to let these moments come to you when they are ready, rather than driving yourself toward them uninvited.

JUST LET GO.
LET GO OF HOW
YOU THOUGHT
YOUR LIFE SHOULD BE,
AND EMBRACE THE LIFE
THAT IS TRYING TO WORK
ITS WAY INTO YOUR
CONSCIOUSNESS.
—CAROLINE MYSS

Fork in the Road

REMEMBER WHAT YOU THOUGHT YOUR LIFE WOULD TURN OUT TO BE when you thought about it as a child. Where did you think you'd be? What did you think you'd be doing? Now, describe where you are and what is different now that you are an adult. Are you happy with where you are? Disappointed? Choose moments or characteristics of your life now that you wish you could show your younger self with pride.

IT AIN'T WHAT
THEY CALL YOU,
IT'S WHAT YOU
ANSWER TO.

—W. C. FIELDS

WHAT'S IN A NAME?

WHAT DO YOU ANSWER TO? Not just in name, but what forms of communication do you find yourself responding to that perhaps you shouldn't? When someone speaks to you in anger or condescension, do you shrink, get angry in return, or feel unfazed? Position yourself in a place of power. How do you want people to speak to you? Consider what it would feel like to respond in a way that deflects that negative behavior, that holds true to what's in your heart.

Authenticity

BE TRUE TO YOUR AUTHENTIC SELF. When has your respect for yourself guided you into a better position, a better choice, or a feeling of greater confidence? When has a lull in self-esteem counteracted it? Pull out some of the emotions you felt in the first situation. How can you use these as anchors for when you need them the next time?

OUR SELF-RESPECT
TRACKS OUR CHOICES.
EVERY TIME WE ACT IN
HARMONY WITH OUR AUTHENTIC
SELF AND OUR HEART,
WE EARN OUR RESPECT.
IT IS THAT SIMPLE.
EVERY CHOICE MATTERS.

—DAN COPPERSMITH

You owe yourself

THE LOVE THAT YOU
SO FREELY GIVE OTHERS.

—UNKNOWN

LOVE TO LOVE YOU

BEING GENEROUS TO OTHERS WITH LOVE and friendship can come easily. We are energized by the relationships we build, and sometimes diffused by them, too. In what ways have you been generous to your own heart, and in what ways have you let it down? Show yourself the love you need to feel.

You aren't
doing "NOTHING"
when you choose to
put your well-being first.
IN FACT, THIS IS THE KEY
TO HAVING EVERYTHING.

—BRITTANY BURGUNDER

NOTHING TO EVERYTHING

TAKING CARE OF YOURSELF NEEDN'T BE A PRODUCTION. What types of doing "nothing" are in fact doing everything for your well-being? How do these moments help you recharge so you are feeling your best self?

Shadow Glow

WHEN IT IS DARK AND GLOOMY, SHADOWS CREEP IN. But from behind those shadows is a source of light. Inspect the light, its glowing rays that impossibly stretch into the edge of darkness. Imagine this light source is your very own. What about it has such power? What elements of your light fend off the darkness?

Most of the
shadows of this life
ARE CAUSED BY
STANDING IN ONE'S
OWN SUNSHINE.

—RALPH WALDO EMERSON

WHEN YOU RECOVER OR DISCOVER
SOMETHING THAT NOURISHES
YOUR SOUL AND BRINGS JOY,
CARE ENOUGH ABOUT YOURSELF TO
MAKE ROOM FOR IT IN YOUR LIFE.

—JEAN SHINODA BOLEN

Dream Discoveries

DELIGHT IN SELF-DISCOVERY. What surprises have come your way, whether as a reminder of something from the past, or small moments that make your heart flutter? When have you made excuses not to do something that brings you more tranquility? How can you welcome it into your world?

A LOVING HEART
is the beginning
of all knowledge.

—THOMAS CARLYLE

YOU ARE LOVABLE

IN THE HEARTS BELOW, consider the ways your heart is capable of offering and accepting love. Write the ways you believe yourself to be *lovable*—not by others, but by yourself. Include the ways you can share that love with those around you. How much love is in your heart to share with the world around you?

ABOUT THE AUTHOR

NADIA HAYES works as a wellness coach in the Houston area. She recharges by writing, knitting, and communing with nature.

ALSO BY NADIA HAYES

CHOOSE CALM

A JOURNAL FOR SOOTHING ANXIETY, BREATHING IN, AND LETTING GO

NADIA HAYES